BETWEEN THE FAIRS

25 YEARS OF AMERICAN ART, 1939-1964

by John I. H. Baur

with a foreword by Lloyd Goodrich

PUBLISHED FOR THE Whitney Museum of American Art
BY FREDERICK A. PRAEGER, *Publishers* / New York · Washington · London

FREDERICK A. PRAEGER, Publishers
111 Fourth Avenue, New York, N.Y., 10003
77-79 Charlotte Street, London W. 1, England

Published in the United States of America in 1964
by FREDERICK A. PRAEGER, Inc., Publishers

Designed by Peter Oldenburg. Printed in the United States of America
by Publishers Printing-Rogers Kellogg Corporation, New York

FOREWORD

THE QUARTER-CENTURY between the New York World's Fairs of 1939/40 and 1964/65 has been one of the most vital periods in the art of the United States. The preceding quarter-century, from 1914 to 1939, had seen many innovations: the realistic revolt against academic idealism, the first wave of modernism, and the opposing movements of regionalism, the American scene, and the social school. But as the 1930's ended, all these movements had run their courses, although they still had their vigorous individual exponents.

The twenty-five years from 1939 to 1964 have been dominated by new, radically different forces. The mid-1930's saw the rise of the second wave of abstract art — the wave that reached its height in the 1940's and 1950's, and on which we are still riding. In these years American abstraction expanded into many free and original forms, more and more independent of European sources. Then came that uniquely American product Pop art, using the everyday banalities of our civilization to create an art that is both funny and devastating, and at the same time reveals a search for a new esthetic order. In these successive inventions the artists of the United States were for the first time making unmistakably original contributions to the international art scene, and were receiving corresponding recognition abroad.

Aside from such dominant trends, American art of the quarter-century, as John Baur makes clear, was marked by a wide variety of cross-currents and of individual viewpoints, ranging from traditional to advanced. This pluralistic diversity, so characteristic of our art, can be seen as the appropriate expression of a democratic society.

The Whitney Museum's exhibition "Between the Fairs: 25 Years of American Art, 1939-1964," and the present publication which grew out of it, are designed to present a survey of this vital and varied period, as represented by some of its leading figures. Many other artists, of course, deserved to be included, had space permitted. About two-thirds of the works exhibited were lent by museums and private collectors, the other third being drawn from the Museum's own collection.

The Whitney Museum wishes to record its sincere gratitude to the owners whose generosity made the exhibition possible, and whose names are given below.

LLOYD GOODRICH, Director
Whitney Museum of American Art

LENDERS TO THE EXHIBITION

Albright-Knox Art Gallery, Buffalo; The American Legion, Alonzo Cudworth Post No. 23, Milwaukee; The Art Institute of Chicago; Mr. and Mrs. Charles B. Benenson, Scarsdale, N. Y.; Dr. and Mrs. Melvin Boigon, New York; Grace Borgenicht Gallery, New York; Mr. and Mrs. Sol Brody, Philadelphia; Mr. and Mrs. William A. M. Burden, New York; Leo Castelli Gallery, New York; Commerce Trust Company, Kansas City, Mo.; The Galleries of Cranbook Academy of Art, Bloomfield Hills, Mich.; Dallas Museum of Fine Arts; Mr. and Mrs. Rodolphe Meyer de Schauensee, Devon, Pa.; Des Moines Art Center; The Downtown Gallery, New York; Durlacher Bros., New York; Forum Gallery, New York; Mr. and Mrs. B. H. Friedman, New York; General Motors Research Laboratories, Warren, Mich.; Graham Gallery, New York; Mr. and Mrs. George Greenspan, New York; Mrs. Edith Gregor Halpert, New York; Harry G. Haskell, Jr., Wilmington, Del.; Joseph M. Hirshhorn, New York; Dr. and Mrs. Cranston Holman, New York; Joslyn Art Museum, Omaha; Lincoln Kirstein, New York; The Knoedler Galleries, New York; Samuel M. Kootz Gallery, New York; Kraushaar Galleries, New York; William H. Lane Foundation, Leominster, Mass.; Mr. and Mrs. Alexander Lerner, Scarsdale, N. Y.; Mr. and Mrs. Albert A. List, New York; Mrs. H. Gates Lloyd, Haverford, Pa.; Marlborough-Gerson Gallery, New York; Pierre Matisse Gallery, New York; Munson-Williams-Proctor Institute, Utica, N. Y.; Museum of Fine Arts, Springfield, Mass.; University of Nebraska Art Galleries, Lincoln; Mr. and Mrs. Roy R. Neuberger, New York; Barnett Newman, New York; Nordness Gallery, Inc., New York; Norton Gallery and School of Art, West Palm Beach, Fla.; Georgia O'Keeffe, Abiquiu, N. M.; Gordon Onslow-Ford, Inverness, Cal.; Betty Parsons Gallery, New York; The Phillips Gallery, Washington, D. C.; Mr. and Mrs. Alexander Rittmaster, Woodmere, N. Y.; Sara Roby Foundation, New York; Mr. and Mrs. John D. Rockefeller 3rd, New York; Paul Rosenberg and Co., New York; Nathaniel Saltonstall, Boston; Mr. and Mrs. James S. Schramm, Burlington, Iowa; Mr. and Mrs. Robert C. Scull, New York; Estate of John Sloan; Stable Gallery, New York; Staempfli Gallery, New York; Mr. and Mrs. Robert D. Straus, Houston, Texas; Wadsworth Atheneum, Hartford, Conn.; Walker Art Center, Minneapolis; Washington University, St. Louis; Mr. and Mrs. Ben F. Williams, Raleigh, N. C.; Mrs. Ferry Marquand Young, Boston.

The Whitney Museum is also grateful to the following for making color plates available for this publication: Art in America; Art News; Arts Magazine; Mr. and Mrs. Sol Brody; William H. Lane Foundation; The Museum of Modern Art; Mr. and Mrs. Roy R. Neuberger; Mr. and Mrs. Robert C. Scull.

INTRODUCTION

THE CREATIVE ASPECTS of American art have never been confined within the boundaries of a single trend or movement during our century. This seems obvious if one looks back to the early decades when such diverse painters as Sloan and Weber, Marin and Sheeler, Hartley and Stella — to mention only a few — were exploring their quite different paths. It is apparently less obvious today, both to those critics who cling to traditional values and to those who champion the avant garde.

The accelerating rate of change in American art during the past quarter-century has sharpened the conflict between styles and attitudes and has tended to force the spectator into more ardently partisan positions. The least popular critical stance today is that of catholicity. Yet it is difficult to see how one can escape the conclusion that the vitality of American art in this period resides as much in the ferment of ideas, and their interaction, as it does in the temporary triumph of one over another. The pattern is, of course, complicated. Some movements rise, flourish and are gone in a decade or less. Others persist for generations, often changing in character, absorbing new concepts and generating opposed ones in direct ratio to the militancy or exclusiveness of their own. In this kaleidoscope the terms traditional and avant-garde have ceased to have much meaning. Movements radical at their birth have come to conservative, even academic ends. Perhaps this is to be expected; it is the classic pattern of the 19th century. Only in our own age has the reverse occurred and a traditional form of art become the avant-garde trend of the moment.

Rapidity of change has had another, rather odd effect on our art. It has often happened that one or two leading figures have outlived the trend they helped to found, yet have produced their best work after their ship has, so to speak, sunk beneath them. We then have the paradox of a movement giving birth to some of its strongest expressions at a time when it has ceased to exist as a movement.

Romantic realism is probably the oldest current in American art, and it illustrates the latter point. Its roots go deep into the 19th century, at the end of which it flowered brilliantly in the work of Winslow Homer. Still vigorous in the early years of the 20th century, it produced men like John Sloan, now dead, Edward Hopper, Isabel Bishop and Raphael Soyer, all of whom are painting today. But among artists of the younger generation, there is scarcely one of any stature who has been drawn in this direction. As a movement it has virtually ceased to exist, yet Hopper, Bishop and Soyer have probably done their finest work during the years of its decline; to ignore them now, simply because the kind of painting they represent no longer seems viable, is to impoverish our concept of what is creative at this moment.

A somewhat similar situation exists in relation to traditional sculpture, except that its roots go back to antiquity. In 19th-century America, however, the classical ideals of Greek art had been watered down into neo-classicism, and the old technique of direct carving — that singularly close relationship between the artist and his material — had virtually disappeared. When William Zorach and José de Creeft, followed a little later by Oronzio Maldarelli and Chaim Gross, revived the twin traditions, they were innovators as well as conservators. Perhaps this explains why their work has, in itself, creative freshness but why, at the same time, it has not inspired a large creative following. One cannot continue to rediscover a great tradition when it has already been so ably re-explored.

Social comment — the expression in art of strong views on justice, poverty, labor and other aspects of man as a social being — was born of the economic depression in 1929, and flourished through the decade of the thirties, after which it perceptibly waned. In this case, however, nearly all of the figures who led the movement during its heyday are still working and are still concerned with the concept of art as a social instrument and a moral weapon in the struggle for democratic values. What has happened is that the followers, the adapters, and the minor figures, have fallen away. One might say that this has strengthened the movement, rather than weakened it, but here, too, no younger painters, since Jack Levine, have made any significant contribution. Reginald Marsh (always somewhat apart from the others) has died, and the strength of the movement still resides in work of the founders: Ben Shahn, Philip Evergood, Robert Gwathmey, Jacob Lawrence and a few others. The related American Scene painting, which also flourished in the thirties, has dwindled even more severely, due in part to the early death of two of its leaders, Grant Wood and John Steuart Curry. Only Thomas Benton, of the original "Triumvirate," remains.

Perhaps the most persistent movement of our modern art has been expressionism, the free distortion of visual reality to convey emotion. Stemming from the then radical innovations of the French Fauves and the German expressionists early in the century, it became one of the main branches of American avant-garde art in the years following the Armory Show of 1913. Among the early pioneers were men like John Marin, Marsden Hartley, George Grosz, Walt Kuhn, Yasuo Kuniyoshi, Max Weber and the sculptor, Bernard Reder, all of whom worked well into our period and all of whom are now gone. A middle generation, including Abraham Rattner, Lee Gatch, Franklin Watkins, Everett Spruce, Rico Lebrun and Doris Caesar has given the movement new vitality during the last twenty-five years, while several younger artists such as Hyman Bloom, Leonard Baskin, Milton Hebald and Elbert Weinberg may well carry it into a quite distant future. But its very age — over half a century — together with the large number of its adherents, has inevitably changed the complexion of the movement from radical to not quite but almost conservative. The extraordinary durability of expressionism may be due to the fact that it is not really a stylistic trend as much as it is a romantic philosophy broad enough to embrace many styles and to stimulate many changing personal interpretations.

Surrealism — the systematic exploration of dream, hallucination and the subconscious mind — was another foreign-born movement, which reached America in the 1930's. Never widespread on this side of the Atlantic, its principal figures could be counted on one hand: Yves Tanguy, Joseph Cornell, Kay Sage, Eugene Berman and one or two others. While the movement, if it really was one here, has long been over, its effect has been profound. It won acceptance for fantastic imagery and private visions — a realm which has been explored in varying ways by such artists as Ivan Albright, Charles Burchfield, Edwin Dickinson, Morris Graves, Loren MacIver and Hugo Robus. Beyond this, it contributed importantly, as we shall see, to the birth of abstract expressionism.

Still another movement which seemed quite radical at its birth, and has now dwindled into a more conservative old age, is that sometimes called Precisionism — a wedding of native realism with cubist design, which produced a semi-abstract art of sharp contours, simplified volumes, often flat, unmodulated colors. Founded in the 1920's by a group including Charles Demuth, Joseph Stella, Georgia O'Keeffe and Charles Sheeler, joined later by Niles Spencer, Ralston Crawford and others, it represented a kind of acclimatization of abstract art to the American scene and the American tradition. Only O'Keeffe, of the founders, is still active, but the influence of Precisionism, like that of surrealism, has ramified beyond its own borders. Something of its hard, precise nature has reappeared in the work of certain extreme realists, such as Paul Cadmus, Jared French, Bernard Perlin, Honoré Sharrer and George Tooker. Something of its crisp, highly organized design is apparent in the more abstract art of Stuart Davis (with its equally American flavor) and perhaps in the linear patterns of Jimmy Ernst.

Abstract art, since the Armory Show, has fluctuated as a force in American art, but all in all it has been the most persistent, vigorous and self-renewing movement of these years. Actually it comprises a number of movements. Geometrical abstraction, like that of Fritz Glarner and Moholy-Nagy, came out of European experiments with purely formal relationships (e.g., Mondrian and the Bauhaus). By the late 1940's, however, Barnett Newman and Mark Rothko began to break the formal mold, creating a new kind of geometry in which mystery and illusion largely replaced the clarity and other classical virtues of the earlier style. Joseph Albers and Ad Reinhardt became important figures in this development from about 1950. Albers, who had long worked in the Bauhaus tradition, demonstrates the shift of values as his work moved from relatively static relationships into color dynamics, where subtle pulsations and movements of color suggest an inner, breathing life. Today Kenneth Noland and a growing number of younger painters have given this kind of art the aspect of a major movement, sometimes called hard-edge abstraction — although in fact its edges are often soft.

Geometrical abstraction has played a smaller but an important role in our sculpture. Here it is more difficult to draw the line between a classical and a more romantic geometry, though the distinction still seems valid. Certainly Naum Gabo belongs to the former, Alexander Calder to the latter. Indeed Calder, with his introduction of movement and shifting patterns, might be considered the father of hard-edge abstraction. José de Rivera and Richard Lippold fall somewhere between.

A very different kind of abstraction — abstract expressionism — has been without question the dominant movement in our art for most of the past twenty-five years. Drawing on the free forms of Kandinsky's early work, and those of Miró and Matta, borrowing from surrealism the principle of automatism and a certain anti-esthetic bias, it became an art which was much more than the sum of its sources, a personal and introspective art based on the premise that the gesture of the hand, the very action of painting, could embody emotional and psychological impulses more autobiographical than esthetic in nature. It was forecast to some degree by the "white writing" which Mark Tobey developed about 1935 and the late paintings of Arshile Gorky, starting about 1941. It emerged more clearly in the work of Hans Hofmann from about 1943 and that of Jackson Pollock from about 1947. At almost the same time, or slightly later, its vocabulary was significantly enlarged by a long list of exceptionally able painters: William Baziotes, Paul Burlin, James Brooks, Willem de Kooning, Adolph Gottlieb, Philip Guston, Franz Kline, Conrad Marca-Relli, Robert Motherwell, Kenzo Okada, Richard Pousette-Dart, Theodoros Stamos, Bradley Walker Tomlin, Jack Tworkov and many others.

Five of these painters have died (Gorky, Tomlin, Pollock, Baziotes and Kline), but most of them are still active and in many cases are painting more strongly than ever. A host of younger artists are also engaged in abstract-expressionist work, so in one sense the movement may be considered at or near its apogee. Yet one cannot escape the feeling that today it is partly sustained by its own momentum. Its essential vocabulary has been established for well over a decade and has not been significantly enlarged by any of its younger recruits.

In sculpture there is no precise equivalent to abstract expressionism, perhaps because automatism, accident and even mere spontaneity are virtually impossible for technical reasons. Nevertheless, the free-form, open abstractions of such men as Herbert Ferber, David Hare, Ibram Lassaw, Seymour Lipton, Isamu Noguchi and David Smith share with abstract-expressionist painting a personal calligraphy, a sense of obscure but deeply felt symbolism and a kind of metaphorical relation to organic forms. This has been the dominant sculptural mode of the last fifteen or twenty years, and it continues to enlist the allegiance of many younger men, although again it is doubtful that they have added significantly to the movement.

One reason for the persistent vitality of abstract expressionism has been the complete freedom which it offers to, or imposes on, the artist. It has had no program like that of surrealism, and has not even demanded a consistently abstract approach. Painters like Pollock and de Kooning have periodically returned to the human figure, while sculptors like Theodore Roszak and Richard Stankiewicz have worked consistently with human or organic forms. In painting, again, a sizable group of artists who began as abstract expressionists have moved entirely into the field of landscape and figure painting, although their work is marked by many abstract-expressionist characteristics — particularly spontaneity of handling. In California this has reached the dimensions of a sub-movement, led by Elmer Bischoff, Richard Diebenkorn and the late David Park. Elsewhere a semi-abstract treatment of landscape and the human figure has flourished in the work of numerous individuals who do not constitute a school and are virtually unrelated to abstract expressionism. The paintings of Milton Avery, John Heliker, William Kienbusch, Karl Knaths and Larry Rivers have little in common, but in their individual ways they have enriched our art by the personal nature of their vision.

The outstanding example of a movement which has turned conservative, traditional qualities into an avant-garde expression is Pop art, that rambunctious child of the 1960's. The new realism, as it is also called, has been seen by some critics as an outgrowth of abstract expressionism, and it is true that painters like Jasper Johns and Robert Rauschenberg owe much to the earlier movement. But on the whole Pop art seems more a revolt against abstract expressionism than a development out of it. Much of it is funny, like Marisol's witty sculpture, and is thus opposed to the seriousness of abstract expressionism. Much of it is anonymous in technique and is thus opposed to the personal calligraphy of abstract expressionism. All of it proclaims the importance of subject, for this is today's Ash Can school, the impolite genre painting of our time — an art that comments on, or rather reflects, such aspects of modern civilization as cafeteria fare (Claes Oldenburg) or billboard advertising (James Rosenquist). Some Pop art, like some Dada art before it, uses actual, machine-made objects, or their facsimiles, with little alteration; it is difficult to find in these works much more than an anti-esthetic gesture. Other Pop artists (Rauschenberg at times) transform their raw materials into designs so handsome that one nearly forgets the tawdry objects of which they are composed — and then there seems little point in using them. The best Pop art walks an artistic tightrope, on one side preserving the associations of its commonplace subjects or materials, on the other side transforming them into esthetically meaningful works of art. The manner of transformation may be a gross enlargement (which can produce startling formal and visual effects, as in Oldenburg's work); it may be the double planes and abrupt color shifts which Rosenquist uses so deftly; or it may be the brilliant play between a formal and fluid design that one so often finds in Rauschenberg's constructions. The art that results may be deadpan and impersonal, but it has an impact beyond that of the shock value of the subject.

The spontaneous explosion of Pop art all over the country during the last few years raises the possibility that it may become a movement of considerable duration and importance, not just a two-day marvel. It is the first "realist" reaction against abstract expressionism which is not primarily conservative in spirit and which seems to have the vitality to hold its own in the present confrontation. Hard-edge abstraction has possibly made as great if less spectacular gains in recent years, but it, too, is in some degree a reaction against abstract expressionism and shares with Pop art a certain objectiveness of spirit and impersonality of manner. Neither wears its heart on its sleeve. Both have generated much enthusiasm among younger painters.

No one can predict the future courses of our art. The conservative critics who long and hopefully foresaw a "return to sanity" from abstraction have not exactly embraced Pop art. The avant-garde critics, who once proclaimed that the "representational art of our day is unredeemable" must feel at least ambiguous about the present enthusiasm for enlarged comic strips and billboards. But the artists go their own ways, each convinced of the eternal principles on which he builds. We are the richer — if sometimes the more confused.

JOHN I. H. BAUR, Associate Director
Whitney Museum of American Art

LASZLO MOHOLY-NAGY

Space Modulator. 1938-40. Oil. 47 x 47.

Whitney Museum of American Art, gift of Mrs. Sibyl Moholy-Nagy.

GRANT WOOD

Parson Weems' Fable. 1939 .Oil. 38 x 50.

Collection of Ferry Marquand Young.

THOMAS H. BENTON

Hailstorm. 1940. Tempera. $32\frac{1}{8}$ x $39\frac{1}{8}$.

Joslyn Art Museum, Omaha, Neb.

EUGENE BERMAN

Daughters of Fire. 1942. Oil. 53¾ x 45.

The Knoedler Galleries.

JOSEPH STELLA
The Brooklyn Bridge:
Variation on an Old Theme.
1939. Oil. 70 x 42.
Whitney Museum of American Art.

IVAN LE LORRAINE ALBRIGHT
That Which I Should Have Done I Did Not Do.
1931-41. Oil. 97 x 36.
The Art Institute of Chicago.

EDWIN DICKINSON
Shiloh. 1940. Oil. 36 x 32.

Graham Gallery.

MAX WEBER
Exotic Dance. 1940. Oil. 30 x 40.

Collection of Mr. and Mrs. James S. Schramm.

RALSTON CRAWFORD

Grain Elevators from the Bridge. 1942. Oil. 50 x 40.

Whitney Museum of American Art,
gift of the Friends of the Whitney Museum of American Art.

MARSDEN HARTLEY

Mount Katahdin, Autumn, Number 1. 1942. Oil. 30 x 40.

University of Nebraska Art Galleries, F. M. Hall Collection.

ARTHUR G. DOVE

That Red One. 1944. Oil. 27 x 36.

William H. Lane Foundation.

MORRIS GRAVES
In the Air. 1943. Watercolor. 26½ x 30¼.

Collection of Mr. and Mrs. Ben F. Williams.

JOHN MARIN
Tunk Mountains, Autumn, Maine. 1945.
Oil. 25 x 30.

The Phillips Collection, Washington, D. C.

ARSHILE GORKY   Betrothal, II. 1947. Oil. 50¾ x 38.

Whitney Museum of American Art.

EDWARD HOPPER

Seven A.M. 1948. Oil. 30 x 40.

Whitney Museum of American Art.

GEORGE GROSZ

Peace, II. 1946. Oil. 47 x 33¼.

Whitney Museum of American Art.

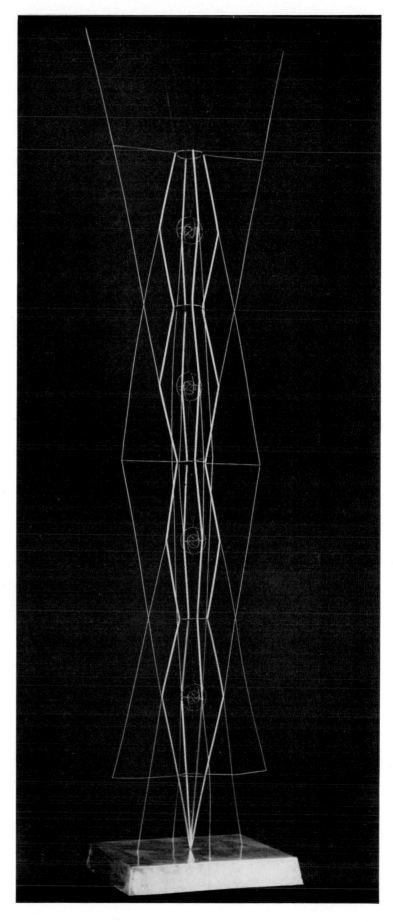

RICHARD LIPPOLD

Primordial Figure. 1947-48. Brass and copper wire. 96 high.

Whitney Museum of American Art, gift of the Friends
of the Whitney Museum of American Art, Charles Simon and purchase.

ANDREW WYETH   Karl. 1948. Tempera. 30⅝ x 23⅝.

Collection of Mr. and Mrs. John D. Rockefeller 3rd.

YVES TANGUY

Fear. 1949. Oil. 60 x 40.

Whitney Museum of American Art.

REGINALD MARSH
Coney Island Beach, 1947.
Egg tempera. 30¼ x 48.

Wadsworth Atheneum, Hartford.

RICHARD POUSETTE-DART
The Magnificent. 1950-51. Oil. 86¼ x 44.

Whitney Museum of American Art,
gift of Mrs. Ethel K. Schwabacher.

LOREN MacIVER
Venice. 1949. Oil. 59 x 93.
Whitney Museum of American Art.

MARK TOBEY
Universal Field. 1949. Tempera and pastel. 28 x 44.
Whitney Museum of American Art.

RAOUL HAGUE

Walnut. 1949. 45 high.

Collection of Mr. and Mrs. Roy R. Neuberger.

SAUL BAIZERMAN

Slumber. 1948. Hammered copper. 40 long.

Whitney Museum of American Art.

HONORE SHARRER

Tribute to the American Working People
(center section). 1951. Oil. 33¼ x 27.

Sara Roby Foundation.

FRITZ GLARNER   Relational Painting. 1949-51. Oil. 65 x 52.

Whitney Museum of American Art.

PHILIP EVERGOOD
The Jester. 1950. Oil. 72 x 96.
Collection of Mr. and Mrs. Sol Brody.

JACQUES LIPCHITZ
Sacrifice, II. 1948-52. Bronze. 49¼ high.

Whitney Museum of American Art.

YASUO KUNIYOSHI
Amazing Juggler. 1952. Oil. 65 x 40¼.

Des Moines Art Center.

ATTILIO SALEMME

Inquisition. 1952. Oil. 40 x 63.

Whitney Museum of American Art.

JACKSON POLLOCK
Number 27. 1950. Oil. 49 x 106.
Whitney Museum of American Art.

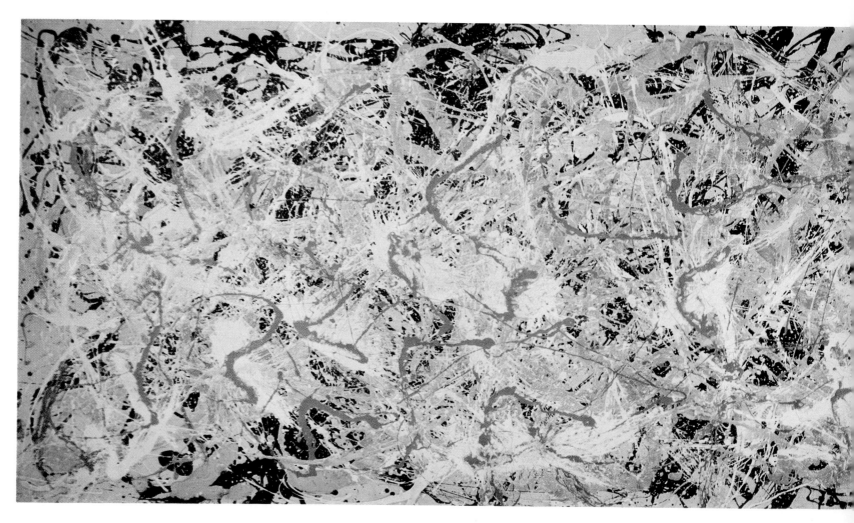

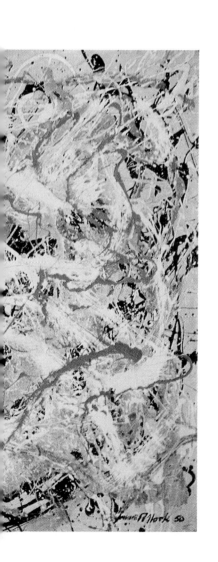

BEN SHAHN
Everyman. 1954. Tempera. 72 x 24.
Whitney Museum of American Art.

RAPHAEL SOYER
The Brown Sweater. 1952. Oil. 50 x 34.
Whitney Museum of American Art.

JOSEPH CORNELL
Hôtel du Nord. c. 1953. Construction
in wood, glass, and paper. 19 x 13¼.
Whitney Museum of American Art.

JACK LEVINE

Gangster Funeral. 1952-53. Oil. 63 x 72.

Whitney Museum of American Art.

LEE GATCH

The Greenhouse. 1950. Oil. 44 x 36.

Collection of Mr. and Mrs. Roy R. Neuberger.

JOSEF ALBERS

Homage to the Square: "Ascending." 1953. Oil. 43½ x 43½.

Whitney Museum of American Art.

MILTON AVERY

The Seine. 1953. Oil. 41 x 50.

Whitney Museum of American Art.

BALCOMB GREENE

Composition: The Storm. 1953-54.
Oil. 36¼ x 48.

Whitney Museum of American Art.

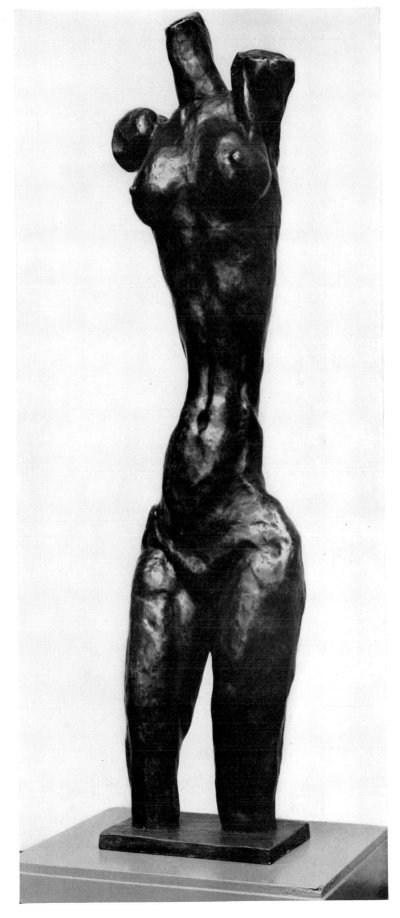

DORIS CAESAR
Torso. 1953. Bronze. 58 high.
Whitney Museum of American Art.

STUART DAVIS

Colonial Cubism. 1954. Oil. 45 x 60.

Walker Art Center, Minneapolis.

LYONEL FEININGER

Fenris Wolf. 1953-54. Oil. 20½ x 30½.

Collection of Mr. and Mrs. Robert D. Straus.

KAY SAGE

No Passing. 1954. Oil. 51¼ x 38.

Whitney Museum of American Art.

CHARLES BURCHFIELD

Night of the Equinox. 1917-55.
Watercolor. 40 x 52.

Sara Roby Foundation.

I. RICE PEREIRA

Landscape of the Absolute. 1955.
Oil. 40 x 50.

Whitney Museum of American Art,
gift of Richard Adler.

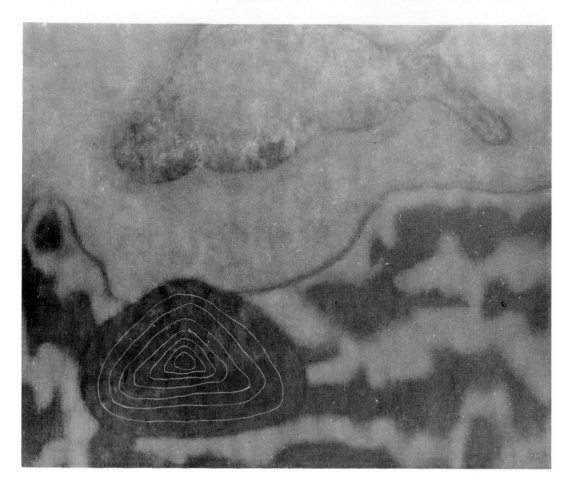

WILLIAM BAZIOTES

Moby Dick. 1955.
Oil. 60 x 72.

Collection of Mr. and Mrs. William A. M. Burden.

ROBERT MOTHERWELL

Je t'aime, II. 1955. Oil. 54 x 72.

Collection of Mr. and Mrs. B. H. Friedman.

PHILIP GUSTON
Dial. 1956. Oil. 72 x 76.
Whitney Museum of American Art.

JIMMY ERNST
Timescape. 1956. Oil. 36 x 48.

Sara Roby Foundation.

CHARLES SHEELER
General Motors Research. 1956. Oil. 48 x 30.

General Motors Research Laboratories, Warren, Mich.

FRANZ KLINE

Mahoning. 1956. Oil. 80 x 100.

Whitney Museum of American Art,
gift of the Friends of the Whitney Museum of American Art.

THEODOROS STAMOS

High Snow — Low Sun, II. 1957. Oil. 53½ x 97½.

Whitney Museum of American Art,
gift of the Friends of the Whitney Museum of American Art.

KENZO OKADA

Memories. 1957. Oil. 68 x 84½.

Whitney Museum of American Art.
gift of the Friends of the Whitney Museum of American Art.

KARL KNATHS
Net Mender. 1957.
Oil. 60 x 42.

The Phillips Collection,
Washington, D. C.

IBRAM LASSAW
Counterpoint Castle. 1957. Bronze and copper. 38 high.

Samuel M. Kootz Gallery.

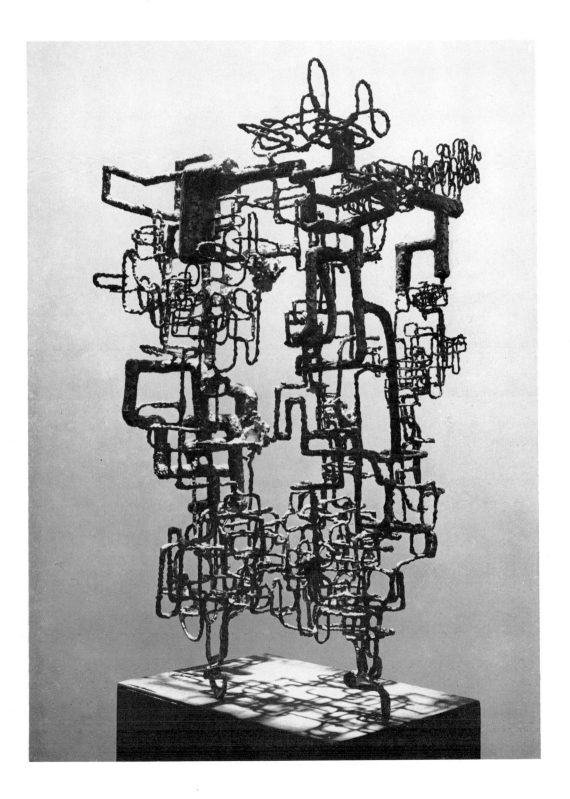

DAVID PARK

Four Men. 1958. Oil. 57 x 92.

Whitney Museum of American Art, gift of an anonymous foundation.

SEYMOUR LIPTON

Sorcerer. 1957. Nickel-silver on monel metal. 60¾ high.

Whitney Museum of American Art,
gift of the Friends of the Whitney Museum of American Art.

NAUM GABO

Linear Construction in Space, Number 4. 1958. Plastic and stainless steel. 40 high.
Whitney Museum of American Art, gift of the Friends of the Whitney Museum of American Art.

CONRAD MARCA-RELLI

The Arrival. 1958. Oil and collage. 69 x 70.

Washington University, St. Louis.

PAUL BURLIN

Red, Red, Not the Same. 1959. Oil. 48½ x 72.

Whitney Museum of American Art,
gift of Sam Jaffe, Milton Lowenthal, Harry Pinkerson,
Bernard Reis, and Dr. Samuel Ernest Sussman.

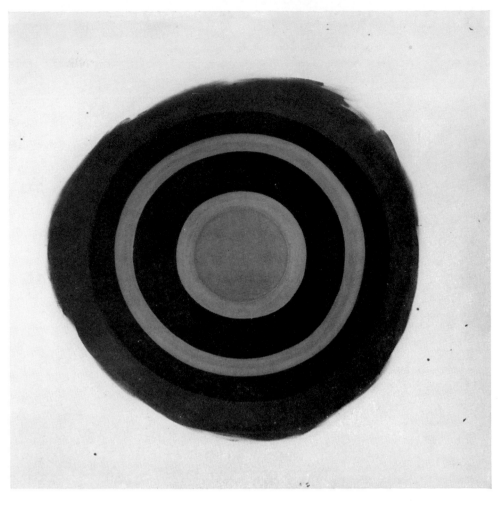

JOSE DE RIVERA
Construction 67. 1959. Forged bronze. 54 long.

Grace Borgenicht Gallery.

KENNETH NOLAND
Song. 1958.
Plastic paint. 65 x 65.

Whitney Museum of American Art,
gift of the Friends of the Whitney Museum of American Art.

LOUISE NEVELSON

Young Shadows. 1959-60. Wood. 115 x 126.

Whitney Museum of American Art,
gift of the Friends of the Whitney Museum of American Art and Charles Simon.

ABRAHAM RATTNER

Song of Esther. 1958. Oil. 60 x 48.

Whitney Museum of American Art,
gift of the Friends of the Whitney Museum of American Art.

JASPER JOHNS

False Start. 1959. Oil. 67¼ x 54.

Collection of Mr. and Mrs. Robert C. Scull.

JAMES BROOKS

Rasalus. 1959. Oil. 66 x 79¾.

Whitney Museum of American Art,
gift of the Friends of the Whitney Museum of American Art.

WILLEM DE KOONING

Door to the River. 1960. Oil. 80 x 70.

Whitney Museum of American Art, gift of the Friends of the Whitney Museum of American Art (and purchase).

ALEXANDER CALDER

The Cock's Comb. 1960. Sheet iron. 159 long.

Whitney Museum of American Art, gift of the Friends of the Whitney Museum of American Art.

ROBERT RAUSCHENBERG

Summer Rental, Number 2. 1960. Oil. 70 x 54.

Whitney Museum of American Art,
gift of the Friends of the Whitney Museum of American Art.

HANS HOFMANN

Sanctum Sanctorum. 1962. Oil. 84 x 78.

Samuel M. Kootz Gallery.

REUBEN NAKIAN

Olympia. 1960-62. Bronze. 72 high.

Whitney Museum of American Art,
gift of the Friends of the Whitney Museum of American Art (and purchase).

THEODORE ROSZAK

Night Flight. 1958-62. Steel. 125 long.

Pierre Matisse Gallery.

DAVID SMITH

Lectern Sentinel. 1961.
Stainless steel. 101¾ high.

Whitney Museum of American Art,
gift of the Friends of the
Whitney Museum of American Art (and purchase).

RICO LEBRUN

Night Figures I. 1962. Oil. 92 x 74.

Nordness Gallery, Inc.

LEONARD BASKIN

Hephaestus. 1963. Bronze. 63¼ high.

Whitney Museum of American Art,
gift of the Friends of the Whitney Museum of American Art.

GEORGE TOOKER

Mirror. 1963. Egg tempera. 20 x 18.

Lent by Lincoln Kirstein (courtesy Durlacher Brothers).

GEORGIA O'KEEFFE

Sky Above Clouds II. 1963. Oil. 48 x 84.

Collection of the artist.

LARRY RIVERS

Moon Man and Moon Lady. 1963. Oil. 2 panels: 68 x 48 each.

Marlborough-Gerson Gallery.

MARISOL

Women and Dog. 1964. Wood and mixed media. 91 wide.

Whitney Museum of American Art,
gift of the Friends of the Whitney Museum of American Art.

BERNARD REDER
Harp Player, 11. 1960. Bronze. 84 high.
Whitney Museum of Art.

WILLIAM KIENBUSCH
House, Nova Scotia. 1963. Casein. 31½ x 44¼.
Kraushaar Galleries.

JOHN HELIKER

Maine Interior. 1963. Oil. 50 x 50.

Commerce Trust Company, Kansas City, Mo.

INDEX TO PLATES

PAGE